SOCIAL MEDIA SIMPLE **MARKETING**

HOW TO GUIDE WITH SIMPLE TIPS & STRATEGIES FOR LOCAL SMALL BUSINESS OWNERS

Andre L. Vaughn

COOL FREE BONUSES!

Thank you for investing in this book. As a thank you, I want to offer you some Free Bonuses to further help your small business succeed with simple social media marketing solutions.

-5 PART VIDEO COURSE

-DOWNLOADABLE REPORT

-PRIVATE COMMUNITY

-EXCLUSIVE ACCESS TO THE AUTHOR

Visit the link below to get access to your **FREE Bonuses!**

www.socialmediasimplemarketing.com

INCOME DISCLAIMER. This document contains business strategies, marketing methods and other business advice that, regardless of my own results and experience, may not produce the same results (or any results) for you. I make absolutely no guarantee, expressed or implied, that by following the advice below you will make any money or improve current profits, as there are several factors and variables that come into play regarding any given business.

As with any business endeavor, you assume all risk related to investment and money based on your own discretion and at your own potential expense.

This document may contain affiliate links for some of the recommended products and/or services. This means that if you purchase the recommended product via the link in this book, we are paid a commission by the original vendor.

LIABILITY DISCLAIMER. By reading this document, you assume all risks associated with using the advice given below, with a full understanding that you, solely, are responsible for anything that may occur as a result of putting this information into action in any way and, regardless of your interpretation of the advice.

You further agree that the author or publishing company cannot be held responsible in any way for the success or failure of your business as a result of the information presented in this document.

This publication is designed to provide accuracy in regard to the subject matter covered. In addition, the author has used his efforts in preparing this book. It is sold with the understanding that the author is not engaged in rendering legal, accounting, or other professional services. If legal advice or other assistance is required, the services of a competent professional should be sought.

Dedication

This book is dedicated to the families and friends of Charles Hillman, Jr. and Brian Jordan, Jr. Two great families who lost loved ones that were left to deal with different circumstances

Acknowledgments

There are way too many people to thank that have led me through my long journey. If I failed to mention anyone then I apologize but know that you were a part of my growth process along with many other things which came throughout my life or this process. First and foremost, I must undoubtedly acknowledge the sacrifices that my family has made during my long hours of research, trials, tribulations and writing. Kendra, Andre, Jr. and Jordan I love each of you with every ounce of my heart and I hope that you all know it.

Next I want to take time to acknowledge my mother Magnolia Vaughn. I could write a series of books on our lives and the impact you have had on me and many others. Special thank you to all of my sisters and brother who has been instrumental throughout the years in more ways than they know. Lynn, Randal, Michelle and Denean thank you all for everything that a little brother could have ever needed growing up and through adulthood. Though we never take the time to say it to one another, I love each and every one of you with all of my heart twenty four hours a day seven days a week.

Most people don't usually mention their in-laws but I have to very supportive in-laws Joe and Yvonne Minor have been so encouraging and good to me in so many ways that I can't even begin to count them. Thank You both for EVERYTHING!

The relationships that I have made over the years have been wonderful with many people and it would probably require a few terabytes of data to name them all. But there are a few who have been instrumental in a variety of ways and happen to be some of the most intelligent people that I know and very proud to call them my friends: Clarence Nash, Adrian Barnes, Kelvin Watson, Chris Farrar, Jessie Taylor, Mark Brown & Siyaka Knight. It doesn't get too much better than those guys. At the very minimum, thank you for believing in me and the long brick roads of my journey.

I owe a debt of gratitude to all of my past professors at my alma mater the University of Missouri-St. Louis. Though I didn't have any personal relationships with any of them specifically, the teachings of their specific subject matter were invaluable. A special thanks to the College of Business in particularly Dr. Vicki Sauter (Systems Analysis), Dr. Joseph Rottman (Systems Design), Jim Pandjiris (Finance) and Peggy Lambing (Entrepreneurship). Each of you took me through the "gauntlet" and really made me do something for the very first time consistently: THINK. I took something positive away from each of you and all that I learned at the University of Missouri-St. Louis. Thank you so much to each of you!

Spread The Word NOW!

I'm going to assume that you already have a Facebook and/or Twitter account so please share your thoughts and show some LOVE about *Social Media Simple Marketing* right now.

Also after you read the book DO NOT FORGET to leave a **Review on Amazon** (or wherever you may have purchased it). It will help us provide more value by updating with current & relevant information and reach more business owners as well.

I understand that you may not have time to leave a review but I would REALLY, REALLY appreciate if you took a few minutes to do so.

Who is This Book For?

Social Media Simple Marketing is for local small businesses that are in any phase of their business whether it's a startup, in business for up to 5 years or much longer, Mom and Pop, brick and mortar, etc.

For local small business owners and other entrepreneurs who are struggling with social media marketing concepts for platforms such as Facebook, Twitter, Instagram, Google Plus Local, Pinterest, YouTube, etc.

Social media managers or consultants can benefit from this book to help with their clients' social media platforms and learn about the tools that are suggested in order to be more efficient. Social media changes quickly so a competent professional will appreciate that he or she must keep up with the industry often as well.

Small or medium sized business owners will find complete value in this book because the simplicity of the information available.

What Does This Book Offer?

This book offers a variety of solutions for local small business owners because marketing your business online has never been this simple. Social media marketing can be complicated if you don't know the different strategies that can help your business thrive in your local area.

Knowledge of things such as how many times should you post on Facebook, how many hashtags can you use on Instagram or how location based services can help your business, etc.

Many local small business owners are not using social media accordingly and don't have time to manage the platforms that they use for their businesses and we bring some of those things to light in this book too.

Will Social Media Marketing Hurt My Business?

I can answer this question a few different ways but the most logical answer that I can give is NO. But what if you outsource tasks and have a horrible experience? Now that would garner a different response.

I would like to think that your customers will be inclined to let you know (along with data) that your efforts are helping your business as well.

Other than something that is not in your control, I really couldn't see a reason that it could hurt your business especially more than it could be a tremendous PLUS for it. Your overall bottom line can be improved when your business uses social media marketing.

What Happens If I Don't Use Social Media for My Business?

If you don't use social media and are clueless about other emerging media platforms then you could possibly get left behind to your competitors (in your local area). Maybe your business is awesome without social media marketing.

Have you noticed mobile devices in the hands of your customers? What do you think they are doing with all of the finger movement? That alone spells opportunity if you can think about that for a minute.

If you want your business to at least have a chance to grow and provide more products and services to potential customers, then you may want to use social media marketing and some of its components.

How Soon Will I Get Results?

There are so many factors that could affect the speed of getting instant results. It depends on a number of things but it could take you 1 minute or 24 hours to start seeing results depending on what exactly you are trying to accomplish.

Are you using Instagram to market your business and effectively using hashtags? If so, then you can see engagement quickly. Are you consistently using Facebook's ad platform to target customers in your local area? Chances are you can see results within a 24 hour period.

I wouldn't worry about a time frame more so than I would to be consistent with my marketing efforts and understand that my success would be predicated on a long term marketing strategy.

Table of Contents

"Information technology and business are becoming inextricably interwoven. I don't think anybody can talk meaningfully about one without talking about the other."

Bill Gates

Co-Founder of Microsoft

Introduction

These are very exciting times if you are a local business owner because of the many options available to market your business online. The emergence of social media has been extraordinary to say the least. It has enabled conversations the world over and has become one of the primary ways for doing business for a lot of companies. But so many local businesses have yet to adapt using it or simply not using it correctly.

Social media marketing is literally taking some local small businesses literally from the ground up to having very successful businesses with consistent growth. Those results are not typical for every local small business but it's very exciting for a number of reasons in which we will discuss later.

I started my first business back in 1998 and it was a satellite installation business. I was so giddy and really thought my new business was going places. The direct to home satellite business was booming and I was in it at the right time. I added sales into the business about 1 year later and had a comfortable income for a few years. The reason I mentioned this is because I had the exact mindset of the typical local business owner back then:

1) I couldn't admit that something was missing within my business though traditional marketing was the absolute best way to market my business at the time

2) Happy that I didn't have to punch anyone's clock but my own

3) I handled way too much responsibility on my own within the business and everything including myself suffered from it

4) A bit naïve to internet marketing and I did not want to admit it

I was doing really well at least I thought and so did everyone else. But in reality my actions were all that I knew at the time because my competitors were doing business the same way.

My business did not grow after about 4 or 5 years. I embraced a disease that follow humans in many aspects of their lives. A disease that eventually ran me out of business around the year 2004 and 2005. The 'inability to adapt to change' was the disease in which I am speaking of. I saw the signs and totally ignored them and before you know it I was back to work under someone else's rules in their business.

I tell this story because as a local business owner we can be stubborn and emotionally attached to our business. And when that happens, a business owner can miss the current wave or the right time for to be a difference maker in their community and beyond. Quite frankly, that's exactly what can happen when you implement social media marketing into your business.

I have outlined a number of things through this simple guide such as an explanation of the different social media platforms, examples, actionable tips, strategies and a few others things that can help any local small business entrepreneur use social media marketing efficiently and effectively.

Your customers are on social media waiting for you to introduce your products and/or services. Do you want to continue to ignore them or do you want to take the initiative and have more loyal customers and create lasting relationships?

Chapter 1

The Simplicity of Social Media Marketing

There are many companies that are doing very well with social media marketing these days. The perception is that only the big dogs can succeed in this new wave of doing business which is *so, so, so* false.

Any local small business with the simplest game plan can succeed with social media marketing because it's much easier to be successful in your local market than trying to achieve dominance in a bigger space such as the entire World Wide Web. The competition in your local area is much, much lower. It doesn't matter if you are a local bakery in a city with 100 other bakeries. Your chances of being dominant with social media marketing are astronomical in your own "backyard." Here's why: A large percentage of local small businesses that are involved with social media aren't using it properly anyway!

Your customers are using social media and are also likely using multiple social platforms. Your business has potential customers looking for it within these different platforms. There could be massive amounts of money left on the table without using social media marketing. And if you are using social media, it is very likely that you are not maximizing the use of the platforms consistently and/or efficiently.

Internet Access is Spreading Rapidly

Wherever your business is located throughout the developing world, many of your customers may likely have access to the web. Internet access is becoming simpler by the second and making social media easily accessible. That probably isn't a new revelation to you but as a local small business owner you have to recognize and adapt to it. More and more people even in remote areas are gaining internet access whether it's through fiber optics or via satellite internet service. This is happening all over the world with high frequency. With internet access your customers are a click away from you and looking for your products and services. They are also interested because you may have exceptional customer service and local which is a convenience to them. Most consumers are comfortable with businesses in their own communities.

The Mobile Wave is here to Stay

Mobile is getting bigger by the minute and when you think about all the smartphones that are available you have to assume that many of your prospects have them as well. Mobile marketing can be undoubtedly beneficial for your business and has the power to take it to another level. Your customers have mobile devices and are using them all the time. It virtually consumes their identity to a degree.

When our cell phones are missing we panic as if we are searching for a needle in haystack. In other words, we need and cherish our mobile devices. We rely on them for just about everything because of the internet service and other apps as well. Many people spend countless hours on their mobile devices using specific social media sites for interaction. The use and availability of mobile devices on social sites are limitless in many cases as well.

Most local business owners would probably never think about or realize the importance of mobile marketing as a way to catapult their business. "Social is Mobile and Mobile is Local" and you can't have one without the other if you want to compete locally. Social media sites such as Facebook, Twitter, Instagram, Periscope, Snapchat, WhatsApp and even Pinterest have location based features that can be accessed very easily on mobile devices which can be huge for any local business. I go a little more in depth about this in Chapter 4 but as a local business owner, you should be more conscientious about every aspect of mobile marketing because it's very lethal when combined with social media.

Modern Day Distribution is Incredible

Thirty years ago distribution with just about any medium was way too expensive whether it is was publishing a book, distributing any news source, etc. It was nearly impossible to do those things on a budget. Fast forward to current times and you will see that it's unthinkably accessible.

I categorized distribution into four categories: Easy, Free, Cheap and Targeted.

1) Easy

It is so easy to distribute content now because all you need is internet access and a PC or mobile device. There are many social media sites to access nowadays. They are very easy to use as well.

2) Free

Distributing content is free when you use social media to share with an audience. Therefore, this accessibility if far more effective because most people will opt to use a free tool that they can sign up for by providing simple information such as a user name and an email address.

3) Cheap

This is the one where I always get a reaction of "Huh?" Yes…cheap! Distribution of content can be cheap when using for marketing purposes. This is primarily meant for PPC or Pay per Click Advertising on social media sites. Two of the most effective social media sites for that are Facebook and YouTube. I will cover that later in this book. You may be SURPRISED at how cheap some social media ads can be when using an effective campaign for your local business.

4) Targeted

The most exciting part of distributing content in current times is that it can be targeted. As a business owner only you know who your customers are. After using the analytics from a few of your social media sites (and of course listening to your customers), it gives a clearer understanding who your customers are. In some cases, you will be able to pinpoint exactly where to find these customers also.

Chapter 2

Some are Not All in on Social Media Marketing

Using traditional methods as a means to grow your business

There are some local businesses that are successful using traditional marketing which is quite fine. If your business is doing well with flyers, yellow page ads, TV commercials, newspaper ads and/or word of mouth, then good for you. My question to you is can you scale your business using those same methods? Can you scale your business with those methods and be cost effective? What happens to your bottom line when the cost of you current advertising increases?

There isn't any problems with traditional marketing (so as long you are getting results) but why not jump on the train and add social media marketing methods to the traditional ones to grow your business easier? You will get the most out of your advertising dollars and your overall marketing strategy when you combine social media marketing with traditional methods.

Lack of knowledge of social media marketing

There are many great and innovative local business owners around the world that have built their businesses without social media marketing. Some of them simply lack the knowledge of using social media. They may just be a bit old fashion and don't use computers personally or professionally. There are plenty of reasons or circumstances why this occurs.

Generational businesses are plentiful

Businesses are passed from one generation to the next and the same methods of doing business still exist within some of them. These business owners keep everything in tact such as their advertising that built the business, while others change with the times. That's the way it is when some businesses are handed down. It isn't a bad thing but it could become challenging later in the life cycle of a brick and mortar or any local business.

Most people in general can't adapt to change simply because of 'fear.' It can hinder progress for any human being because it's within all of us whether or not we want to admit it or not. There are many reasons why adapting to social media marketing can scare the heck out of a local business owner. Relax folks….'fear of change' is natural and isn't going anywhere anytime soon along with social media marketing.

No Success Currently Using Social Media

I love lurking around at different small business social media profiles on the web and see how those businesses are using it. It is very interesting how BAD businesses fail to take advantage of building an audience on the different social platforms. Don't feel bad because some of the big brands SUCK even worse than the local or small businesses do!

Many local businesses are simply not using social media correctly. It can be a simple process if embraced...not difficult at all. Just because you have a Facebook fan page with 'Likes' doesn't mean anything if you are not managing it properly and utilizing it to the fullest.

Chapter 3

A Different Mindset Is Needed ASAP

Business Owners must Stop being Emotionally Attached

Plenty of local business owners are so emotionally attached to their business that it may affect their ability to scale their operations. Through my experiences as a business owner, my stubbornness cost me several thousands of dollars because I was too caught up into the "Machismo" style of owning a business. The "it's my own business" and "I do what I want" syndrome. Sometimes stepping back and relinquishing some responsibility can help your business grow immensely.

You Can't do it All By Yourself

As a local business owner you have to deal with the day to day operations and different aspects related to your business. This is a trait most business owners have which may propel you to be hands on and in many cases too much for you. Business doesn't have to be done this way anymore.

Social media management can be outsourced very easily. That responsibility can be given to someone else for a very low fee. Once you train someone to do this, you will see that it may cost you more in terms of time and productivity NOT to outsource this (and other functions of your business too). I dive more into this concept so that you can have a better understanding of it in Chapter 14. You may not be able to do everything in your business alone and grow it in the process.

Must build your Audience First

For a local business owner, the concept of building an audience first might just be unheard. The notion that one has to get a bunch of people to like their product and services before doing anything else is quite foreign to some. The mind shift can be a difficult task.

If you build your social channels first with raving fans, it can mean the difference between a five figure business a year to a six figure business a year! Give value (a lot of it) first, and the dynamics of your business can grow at an awesome pace if these principles are implemented properly (assuming your products or services are in demand). These results are not typical but what if your business only DOUBLED would that be ok with you? How about TRIPLED?

Stop Believing that Social Media Cannot be Monetized

Monetizing social media can be accomplished just as anything else in business. Knowledge of these different web based applications and the functionality of them can propel your business to another level if you are willing to learn, believe and provide value in the process. There's something about "New" that correlates to "uncharted waters" sort of speak for some.

Many businesses are doing well because they have learned the most effective ways to maximize their profits through social media marketing. Without question monetization can occur for your local business if you are more than willing to learn and accept how simple many of the social media platforms are to implement effectively.

Integrate with Current Marketing Efforts

It's very important to continue your current marketing campaigns only if they are working for your business. The idea is not for you to relinquish all of your current advertising, but to simply integrate social media marketing slowly (which is why I previously spoke about building your audience first).

You can integrate with social media very smoothly by doing a simple thing such as adding your social media addresses on marketing materials or adding it on your printed receipts. Being able to combine social media efforts with current marketing will do a lot for the overall mindset of a local business owner and increase brand awareness in the process.

Chapter 4

Benefits of Social Media for Local Businesses

New Customers Are Waiting For You

One of the benefits of social media is that just about everyone (relatively speaking) is using some type of social platform or even multiple platforms. It has become a way for people to share and comment on just about anything with their friends about anything. There are swarms of new customers waiting on your business. They will talk about it especially if they had a good experience with your products and services.

Customers or potential customers will also speak negatively about your business if they have a bad experience as well. As a local business owner, you must have a plan in place for complaints also. Many of the larger businesses like to engage and take care of customer issues on places like Twitter because of the convenience and ease of the platform.

As of September 2013, **72 percent of online adults** were using social networking sites, according to the Pew Research Center. This is happening over just about every demographic regardless of circumstances. In addition, social media campaigns have been shown to be more effective in generating quality leads. This information spells out opportunity for local businesses.

Build and Engage with Potential Customers

I can't express enough about the importance of building your audience first. Consumers won't buy much if at all when they are not getting your attention. There are many ways of doing this such as sharing great content about your products or by asking questions.

"Great content" may throw some of you off a bit but its simple and here's an example: Let's say that you have a bakery business in your town or city and you have an Instagram page. You already have 1000 plus followers of the page so a fair amount of people will see your posts organically. Instead of always posting about your "Jelly Donuts are 50 cents" on any given morning, its more appropriate to give value by sharing information on "why" the Jelly Donuts are a part of your list of products. You could also discuss the history of the Jelly Donut and how it came about as an example. When users comment on your posts, be sure to respond and answer their questions if needed. Your customers or potential customers love to be engaged and valued so always build trust with them as often as possible.

Show Up in the Search Results

When you set up social profiles, some may show in the search results (search engines like Google, Bing and Yahoo). This is important because you want to be sure that you select the proper title or username when setting up your profile. Start noticing in the URL bar (box that shows "http://www.......com") the name of the user typically after the "....com/social-username." If you set up a social profile page such as "BEST DONUTS IN YOUR CITY" and someone searches "BEST DONUTS IN YOUR CITY," chances are that your profile may appear in the search results among the very first choices for those keywords. This is a great way of getting organic traffic to your social media profile with a little ingenuity on your part.

Mobile Can Be Confusing but Beneficial with Social Media

Some business owners can easily be confused to what exactly mobile marketing consists of because they are told and pitched heavily on mobile apps. I am here to tell you or shall I scream to you: "YOU DO NOT NEED A MOBILE APP AS A LOCAL BUSINESS!"

At least 99% of you don't. I'm not going to explain too heavily on why you don't need it but answer this question, "Who in your local area will know that you have an app and for what purpose will it serve customers that your other mobile optimized properties (website & social media sites) can't?" Or "How often will someone in your area open a mobile app to receive immediate value from your business that they couldn't do on any of your other available platforms on a repetitive basis?"

Local businesses are searched heavily on social media sites such as Facebook, Twitter, Pinterest and even Instagram (in which I go over in more detail later) with mobile devices. The thing to remember is that your social media profiles within these platforms along with a few other important things must be set up properly to enable geo or location features within those mobile platforms.

A local business can also benefit from many other features from a mobile platform that can very easily integrate with social media such as email marketing, text messaging, QR codes, mobile optimized social campaigns (contests, surveys & games) and mobile coupons. The true benefit of mobile is that all of these benefits can be tracked for performance so that a business can see all the available data to make conscious decisions overall.

The benefits can seem endless when mobile is implemented properly with current traditional methods combined with social media. Mobile cannot be ignored any longer so position your local business now and don't wait to benefit from it. You can be the exception amongst your competitors in your local area if you become a first mover and learn how valuable mobile is as an addition to your entire social media marketing strategy.

Chapter 5

Take Full Advantage of the Entire Google Platform

Google Can Help Your Local Business w/Search Results

Google is a very, powerful company online as we all know. Their search engine along with the local division Google My Business (in conjunction with Google Local for users) and even their social media arm Google Plus can help your local business in a major way. Have you ever noticed that when you are searching for anything locally using their search engine that many options in a row with reviews are seen quickly? There are many positives and as you can tell Google loves their own products and they are easily accessible as part of their search algorithm. Quite naturally their products get high priority and visibility in their own search results. Many local businesses thrive because of Google's search results.

The Google Plus Social Network

Google Plus is a social network that can propel your efforts and stock pile a wealth of leads and customers when combined with everything else that I will discuss about the Google platform.

Not surprising to many people but it's one of the top social networks in the world. It is a great community for a local business because of everything else that is connected to it.

'Circles' which means the network that you are in with other users, will get bigger the more that you post quality content. People in your area will organically add you to them. It's very important to share and +1 (Google Plus' way of "Liking") on others posts that may interest you to stay active within the community. As a rule of thumb, be sure to "show love" to other similar businesses in your area by sharing their content more so than yours. It will pay off your business in the long run.

Google loves to integrate their products probably more so than any other social media site and they do an excellent job of it as well. I cannot express enough how important Google Plus is for any local business so please use it because it's also a very simple and helpful social media tool for your business.

Brief Intro to Google My Business

"Big brother" Google has it all and is very effective for many local businesses around the world. *Google My Business* is a very good and effective tool for local businesses that can target local customers by using search and reviews all in one. You must take *full advantage* of this platform!

Did you know over *25%* of all Google searches are intended for local products and services with over *40%* going to all mobile searches? Local businesses have a very high visibility in the Google search algorithm. Ninety seven (*97%*) of all consumers search online for local businesses. Why wouldn't you want increased exposure online for your local business by using the Google My Business?

Three Important Factors for Local Searches with Google

1) The Google search algorithm takes precedent on local searches in your area (i.e. "Local" Donut Shop or Brake Shop, etc.). The results are almost always near the top to middle of the search page for the highest visibility.

2) Google has set up their local search for consumers to find local businesses without too many distractions. Your Google Plus local page will only compete with others and no other websites, etc.

3) Google My Business is a must for any local business because of the listings that will occur in the search engine but more so it's

a place where your customers can leave *reviews* about your products and services. The reviews hold a fair amount of weight within the algorithm so be sure that you are encouraging your customers to leave positive feedback.

Southern California Spa Business Utilizing Google Very Well

A great example of a local business using Google's platform with excellent results is called BodyCentre Wellness Spa in Anaheim, California. This small business has a web and social presence and wanted to boost their exposure and ultimately get more clients through Google + business profile and search results.

"In one month, BodyCentre Wellness Spa went from number four in Google search results to number one, appearing as the top business new customers see when searching for spas in the Anaheim area. They gained a dozen new Google reviews boosting the business' reputation and providing peer reviews that help new customers make an informed decision that drive in-store visits." -LocBox

Simple Bonus Tips for Google Marketing

Always encourage your current customers to leave an honest review on your Google business page. So many local businesses fail to SIMPLY ask their clientele to do so. Reviews rank very heavily on Google and provides social proof for potential customers when it's positive.

Another surefire tip to give your business better rankings is to buy ads through Google AdWords which is their advertising platform. You control how much to spend and I recommend running multiple ads to split test to find which ad converts the best. Combined with everything else that was previously discussed regarding the Google platform, running an ad WILL DEFINITELY BOOST YOUR RANKINGS BECAUSE OF THE GOOGLE ALGORITM!

Chapter 6

Video Marketing is Simple and Effective for Local Businesses

Video marketing is so easy to do and can be highly effective for your business. It sounds like a lot and so technical but it really isn't at all. There are many video sites but the best one for many reasons is YouTube. Google purchased YouTube in 2006 and it has grown into an absolute powerhouse. That's reason enough to use videos to market your local business!

YouTube is the most widely used video site in the world with over 1 billion users. It is also the 2nd largest search engine on the internet behind Google. I know that you are probably thinking "Videos, how can I implement that or how does that help my business?" or even "how is YouTube a social media site?" You should have questions such as those and I will explain.

Videos and photos will get the most reaction out of your potential customers. Think about it for a minute…assuming that you have a profile on social media or simply watching TV you can get "WOW'D" very easily (yes I just made that term up or at least the spelling…HA…HA!). A visual is very impactful because it draws an emotional response whether it's good, bad or entertaining but most of the entire audience shows interest.

YouTube is a social media site too because of the interactions (Likes, Comment, and Shares) of the videos that are made. When a video is produced and distributed properly, engagement usually occurs and users may subscribe to your channel for future content or click on a link if you provide one in the description box. That should have read, "…when you provide a link…" (Hint) and of course you will, right? As a local business (or any business owner), you should ALWAYS add a link in the description box and be sure to add 'http://www.website.com' or the entire hyperlink of your website including the dotcom. Business in your local area is competitive and you want to be first in line and find the right customers for your establishment.

Video production: "How will I do that plus I don't know anything about videos?" I have a very simple answer for your concerns that I will get to in a moment. The interactions that come from videos are crucial for your business because it gives you an opportunity for more business. Each one of these interactions is seen by anyone that follows or "SUBSCRIBES" to the person that just interacted with your video. YouTube is a social media website just like all the others but a very powerful video sharing tool as well.

Producing a YouTube video is a small portion of what you need to know to position your local business ahead of your competitors. I will discuss in three categories as if a budget was created to see how cost effective a simple video can become. I will also suggest the best fit if you are the typical local business based on if you were starting now or assuming that you are an established local business.

1) High Budget

If you have money to burn or just a healthy budget, then you may want to hire a video production crew. There a few good places to find one by simply doing a Google search or just go to Craigslist or Backpage to see if there's anyone offering their services.

2) Low Budget

This method is for people who are starting out that don't have a lot of money or don't want to spend a lot of time on making a video. You can get a 'Nice' video produced for as little as $5 on Fiverr.com. When you go to their website be sure to do a search on "video" or something else pertaining to it like "video production" to see what interests you.

3) Lowest Budget

The most efficient way to produce a video is by recording everything yourself. By doing this you can save money. You may be giving up time but who cares because your costs will be zero unless you have to do something such as purchase proper lighting and editing software for your videos if you are recording indoors. Writing a script (if you chose to do so) will be at zero cost if you are producing your own content.

How Do I utilize Video Marketing?

My preferred way of using YouTube is through the low budget and lowest budget ways. I like whiteboard videos and you can find someone to produce a simple and nice HD video for you on Fiverr. There are countless other options for you on Fiverr so that you can start producing videos easily for your business. I speak more extensively about Fiverr.com in Chapter 13.

I also enjoy making short videos with my iPhone. It's very economical and it yields a zero cost in my expense column. My business doesn't require a lot of glitz and glamour that a big production would bring. You can also opt for something nice like a cartoon type video that can cost a little more ($50-$100 for a really good cartoon). The quality will be great and it will get the attention of potential customers and bring some credibility to a local business if produced properly.

6 Tips for Making Effective Videos

Tip #1 Keep your audience engaged

Simply put, if your audience is not either entertained or if you're not providing something of value (not doing something out of the ordinary such as attempting to jump off of a skateboard or something that is totally outrageous), then just find a way to keep them glued to your video somehow. My advice is to make your videos entertaining and/or by teaching something because they will convert better and the viewer will likely return if you have helped them solve a problem.

Tip #2 Keep your videos short in length

The reason for short videos is to keep your audience interested in your content. Studies have shown that after 3 minutes of footage on most videos, the audience may become disinterested and leave.

Tip #3 Make testimonial videos

When you make testimonial videos for your business it gives you social proof and legitimacy for your business. Real life testimonials about your products or services are the only type that I recommend because people will resonate with that more and it gives credence to your business.

Tip #4 Make videos consistently

This tip gets so over looked because most local business owners will not give it a chance from the beginning. The business owners that will give it a chance will see the true value in a consistent video marketing strategy because it can truly work wonders. The more consistent videos that you make, the more favoritism they will get within the search engines (particularly with YouTube and Google search engines). Remember that these are the TOP 2 search engines in the world so potential customers in your area will be able to find your products and services rather easily.

Tip #5 Enter Keywords in the Title, Descriptions and Tags

In order to target potential customers in your local market, your keywords must be implemented in three areas for success: the title, description and tags. Before you upload any videos on YouTube, it is very important that all three are filled out properly. If they are not, then potential customers in your area will not be able to find you.

Here's a quick example: You are the owner of a great chiropractic practice in Phoenix, AZ and you just made a quick video about a special deal for potential clients for "FREE Consultation Visits for the first Twenty People."

The aforementioned looks like a great start for a title but the search engines will view it as just that, meaning what you have in the current title. But how will your customers find you? The title should read,

"Phoenix, AZ Chiropractor gives FREE Consultation visits for first Twenty People." With adding, "Phoenix, AZ Chiropractor" it will show in the search results for YouTube and possibly Google when 'chiropractors' are searched in the greater Phoenix, AZ area.

Tip #6 YouTube Advertising Platform

Local Man reaches Buyers around the World from his Videos

Some local businesses have expanded throughout the world with no intention of doing so initially. This was the case for an Atlanta, GA man that makes and sells pottery named Charles Smith. He was relying heavily on galleries and art shows to sell his work but now he markets his products by shooting YouTube videos. Now people buy his work from around the world, his videos are FREE and he has ZERO marketing costs from using the YouTube platform!

The example above is rare nowadays with the entire landscape of social media marketing shifting to a 'pay to play' environment especially for new content that doesn't go viral. Google is at the forefront and YouTube has become that type of platform as well. YouTube Ads which are basically like Google Adwords can help get video content seen by potential customers very quickly. They're easy to set up and very effective when video campaigns are built correctly.

Final Words about Video Marketing

I could write forever about the importance of video marketing and how YouTube can be a preferred method for making simple videos for your local business. Remember that YouTube gets preferential treatment by Google because obviously they love their own products which they should.

It is also a great idea to distribute your videos across all of your other social channels. It is very easy to do this by copying the video link into the post of your selected social platform. If you have any issues performing this task then simply do a search on Google or within the specific platform itself and learn how to embed a YouTube video. The reach for your message in your videos will expand which means the potential for more customers.

There are other options to use for video such as Vine but it makes so much sense for a local business to use Google's product (YouTube) for video marketing purposes because of how it is easily integrated with their other products and you can be found in the search engines which is an added benefit. As you can see I am very passionate about how your local business can capture HUGE gains for your business for years to come by integrating video marketing as part of your social media marketing strategy.

BONUS...

Live Streaming, Mobile & Video Messaging

I believe that live video streaming and mobile messaging is here to stay. Seemingly out of nowhere more of these social, mobile, local and video sites have arrived. Apps and/or functions like Periscope, Facebook Live, Blab, Meerkat, Snapchat and WhatsApp have arrived with a vengeance (sort of speak).

I would only focus on three for local business owners and those are Periscope, Snapchat and WhatsApp. The reason I suggested those is when you combine social media with video and location based geo features (which all 3 possess) it becomes a bonafide complete content medium.

Facebook Live is only available for more established accounts which typically includes celebrities or businesses that have a great number of followers or have spent consistent ad dollars over time on Facebook. Meerkat and Blab are generally not used by local small business because of the lack of features that a similar app like Periscope offers.

Periscope is a video live streaming app that was purchased by Twitter before it ever launched in January 2015. What is so neat about it is when you start a live stream or "Scope," it sends an immediate notification to all of your followers. One of the best strategist for this platform is Ray Garcia (@raygcreative) who has a YouTube channel called Periscope 101 with videos for beginners.

Snapchat is currently growing at an alarming rate and is almost like a "behind the scenes" video messaging system that uses location based geo features to show a user's location. As a business you can 'Snap' which is a 10 second video or create a "Story" which is a collection of 'Snaps' to actually tell a story about your products and/or services. Snapchat has some really cool geofilter features to make your videos appealing to potential customers.

WhatsApp which is a cross platform instant messaging app that was purchased by Facebook in February of 2014. A user can send SMS or text messages without paying additional fees through their phone provider. You can also share your location along with photos and most importantly videos. WhatsApp has 1 billion users at the time of publication which is more than enough reason to explore the platform.

Live streaming, mobile and video messaging poses a HUGE opportunity for local small businesses. Get to know the Periscope, Snapchat and WhatsApp video applications to see how they can possibly generate leads and customers for your business.

Chapter 7

Going Local with Pinterest

Pinterest is a great visual tool and currently is one of the fastest growing social media sites as of publication of this book. According to Marketing Land in September of 2015, Pinterest had over 100 million unique monthly visitors, making it one of the fastest site ever to break that mark.

With Pinterest, users build "boards" which they can optimize with the type of business that they have and within the "boards" there are images or videos created called "pins." When you setup your username on this platform please be mindful that (along with the boards and pins) you should want to optimize it for the search engines.

"Place Pins" on Pinterest is a local business dream if done properly. It was designed to combine great images with the use of an online map so that you can share useful information with the use of a mobile device (you can get directions to a business as well). I won't dive too deep into "Place Pins" but I highly encourage you to research it to find out more details.

It's a great opportunity to promote your local business to a BIG audience especially if you are in an industry such as food services or even hospitality. "Pinners" (who are the users within Pinterest) will place these "Pins" on related boards so that their followers can see these visuals and descriptions of your products and services. Don't wait and please take advantage of this NOW before your competitors does it before you!

Three Things that You Should Do on Pinterest

1) Fill Out the "About You" section on the Edit Profile

Your description should contain specific keywords about your business. These are very important because the terms are searchable within Pinterest's algorithm and you want people to find you inside of there. Also within the "Edit Profile" section, be sure to add your Full Address of your business and your website in the "Location" and "Website" sections.

2) Create High Quality Boards

Within the boards, be sure to give long tailed keywords in the title (with the Main Keyword being the first word) to make your products or services stand out more. Also in the description you must add keywords in the first sentence and its good to add them in the final sentence as well. Please do not "keyword stuff" or use your keywords too many times. Make everything look natural within your boards because the algorithm will most certainly take that into consideration. Lastly, be sure to use hashtags (#) at the end of the description of the board so that your keywords can be better searched.

3) Use High Quality Images and YouTube Videos

Remember that Pinterest is a visual discovery tool and it is very important that you use high quality graphics for your business. You don't need anything specialized other than your smartphone or any mobile device that take great pictures in HD. If you are using Instagram or Tumblr then it may be useful for you to connect all of those accounts together to utilize your images from those platforms as well.

When adding "Pins," be sure to embed YouTube videos of your local business. Pinterest has made this function compatible with YouTube and the same rules apply with your main keywords and hashtags (#). Videos work very well with Pinterest and provides an additional way to showcase your local business.

There are so many things that you can do to add value to your local business on Pinterest so please feel free to do more research if needed to better your knowledge on this great social platform.

Wisconsin Local Businesses & the Power of Pinterest

Big Brothers and Big Sisters of Northwestern Wisconsin along with the Mayo Clinic Health System of Eau Claire are utilizing Pinterest as part of their social media strategy. Big Brothers and Big Sisters uses it quite often especially to share ideas with one of their main clients who benefits from it very well. They even plan on using Pinterest with some of their bigger events since its work so well for them. The Mayo Clinic has combined the imagery of Pinterest with Facebook and Twitter to add more power to their overall strategy. They have figured out that quality images and graphics can drive engagement if you tell the story properly with a visual. It helps them connect with their target audience very well.

5 Pinterest Facts

1) Pinterest is one of the most popular social network in the U.S. in terms of traffic behind Facebook, WhatsApp, Facebook Messenger, Tumblr, Instagram, Twitter & Snapchat

2) Pinterest is retaining and engaging users as much as 2-3 times more efficiently than Twitter was at a similar time in its history

3) Over 80% of pins are repins, demonstrating the tremendous "virality" at work in the Pinterest community

4) 75% of Pinterest traffic comes from its mobile app

5) Shoppers referred by Pinterest are 10% more likely to make a purchase than visitors who arrive from other social networks, including Facebook and Twitter

Chapter 8

Why Instagram and Tumblr Can be So Useful for Your Local Business

Most SEO (Search Engine Optimization) experts or local business marketing experts almost NEVER talk about the sheer power of Instagram and Tumblr to catapult their local businesses. I am writing about these two combined because they work so beautifully together.

Both of these social media networks are great visual tools along with Pinterest but are very unique in their own way. To the mainstream, Instagram and Tumblr may be a bit unassuming but can add a little extra punch for your business. I will provide a little history on both and then I will show an example of how Instagram is helping one local business and share a powerful tip that Tumblr provides.

Instagram

Instagram came on the scene like gang busters especially after the company was purchased by Facebook in April 2012 for an estimated $1 billion in cash and stock. What's great about this Instamatic cameras of the 1960's through late 1980's combined with today's High Definition ratio of 16:9 which just about every mobile device has nowadays.

Users are able to record short videos up to 30 seconds. This can work wonders for your products and services. It can make them stand out far above and beyond your competition. According to the great internet marketer and entrepreneur Gary Vaynerchuk, "Instagram is similar to a magazine" and is steadily becoming a resource that all local businesses can be utilizing in some fashion.

The Instagram mobile app is one of the most downloadable apps currently in the marketplace. It's a free app like all the other major social media sites and there are many people available to you as a business owner to target within this platform.

As of the publication date of this book, Instagram has over 400 million monthly active users (2016). Its popularity has steadily shown that people online love a great visual. Way too many local businesses are not taking advantage of it. Instagram has many more tools and features than I will discuss but it can most certainly help any local business immensely.

Successful Local Business Enticing Customers with Instagram

A Columbia, SC clothing shop called Bohemian is putting Instagram to work as part of their social media strategy. They take photos of their merchandise and upload them to Instagram especially when it's clothing that has unique colors or patterns. Their customers will walk in the store directly for those particular items in which they discovered on Instagram and make a purchase. With permission of the customers, Bohemian employees sometimes will take a photo when a customer tries on merchandise and upload it to Instagram. It adds to the overall customer experience and their customers will not only come back again but will refer friends as well. In about three months they had over 1,000 followers and constant visitors to their storefront.

Tumblr

Internet giant Yahoo owns Tumblr which is a microblogging and social networking site that is very popular because of the visual element (over 550 million active monthly users in 2016). It's like the "misunderstood" friend or family member that we all know because most people simply don't understand how it actually works. It is one of the most powerful social media sites today. Yep I said it and you heard me correctly: "...most powerful...today."

I will briefly share with you how it can work for your business in conjunction with Instagram. Your competitors are likely not using Tumblr to target any prospects and if they have an account their likely not actively or aggressively using it. Simply connect your Instagram account to your Tumblr account and when you take a picture or shoot a quick video, it is smoothly shared on your Tumblr account.

Here's why Tumblr is So Powerful

The functionality of Tumblr does something that is seemingly automated more than any other social site: Shares or "Reblogs" as they call it on Tumblr. Content is moving readily through the constant engagement on Tumblr. Go visit the site and setup an account it's very easy to do. Once again be sure to connect your Instagram to your Tumblr account for maximum results.

I have never seen a social site with so many "shares" and "Likes" of content and with the constant consistency as Tumblr (other than Pinterest and Instagram but notice all three are visually related). Not Facebook, Twitter, Google Plus or LinkedIn has the type of engagement that Tumblr will give content on its site.

Quick Tumblr Tip

The reason that most people don't understand Tumblr is unless your content gets action (Reblogs and Likes) then it may get unnoticed. You have to follow people on Tumblr to get noticed, right? Of course you have to follow people but here's a little trick to get targeted traffic to your Tumblr blog (it's a Micro blog and please don't let that throw you off in anyway). Go to the Google search engine and enter "Tumblr tagged Keyword" ("Keyword" being the main word that you are targeting for your business and NOT the actual word "Keyword"...I know that most of you will get it correct but someone will type in the word "Keyword" and expect results...HA...HA...). Look at the search results and click on any of the targeted keywords that show the number of "notes." Scroll down and click on the number with the most notes and start follow all of the people that reblogged and liked the relevant content for your specific "Keyword."

You can only follow 200 per day on Tumblr and it lets you do this function until you reach a follow count of 5,000. The goal is to get 700-1000 followers in return total from this alone. It will only take 25 days consecutively to follow this amount and you will be followed back by 14-20% of the people that you follow which is huge if they are local! Be sure to enter the name of your city with your relevant keywords or otherwise your results will be minimal.

Also, you can reach out to other Tumblr members of your "like minded" niche and form partnerships to share each other's content (if possible). Remember with all social media sites, you must be active in the community by engaging and helping others out as well by reblogging and liking their content as well.

Tumblr's capabilities can become a hidden gem for your local business not only because of the beautiful imagery and videos but because it's truly one of the most engaged communities in social media per content and it will continue to be that way for years to come.

Chapter 9

Local Businesses can Succeed from a Professional Social Network Too!

I personally believe "where there are people with good incomes then opportunities will always be available." I just simply described LinkedIn and how it can be huge for a local business. LinkedIn is a professional social media site with well over 430 million people networking and over 100 active monthly users (according to 2016 data).

LinkedIn should be very exciting for any business owner because you can search for highly targeted customers. All you have to do is go to the top of your LinkedIn home page and click on the "Advanced" link and enter the detailed information. Be sure to fill out the required information to target your ideal customer in your area. This enables you to find exactly the type of customers for your business. Another benefit is the average income of a LinkedIn member is over $100,000! That opportunity alone should be super exciting for any business owner.

One of the Easiest Social Networks for Business

LinkedIn is one of the easiest social networks for any local business and here are four reasons:

1) You can target people in your specific area
2) Average annual income is ripe for most local businesses
3) Members are very informative and helpful
4) Join and Create relevant groups

It wasn't a mistake that I mentioned the first two things twice (target people and average income) in this section and the previous one. I did so because it's a key element in getting people to make connections with you so that your business can be profitable. As a local business owner, I encourage you to take full advantage of this before your competitors do so. Being the first and /or the most consistent can pay huge long term dividends for your business.

Setting up Your Profile is Very Key

You must complete your profile fully when setting up your LinkedIn account. Use keywords for your business when you are completing your profile especially when you are filling out your headings, subheadings and within your summary and experiences sections. It is very important to complete your profile so that others can find you and your business while completing a search on LinkedIn.

Relevant Groups and LinkedIn

I believe that the most overlooked part of LinkedIn are the groups. Be sure to search for relevant groups for your local business. These groups can be a huge resource in getting recognition in your specific area. I recommend that you join as many groups as you can (up to 50 on a free account). One of the reasons for this is that you can possibly target people within the groups in your specific location or nearby.

Also if any of the members in the group are not in your network or you don't have a "1st connection" with them, you can use LinkedIn's internal mail system to connect a potential customer (since you are in the same group with them). LinkedIn groups are a true hidden gem if used properly and most certainly will add value to others that are seeking your products and services.

Advertising on LinkedIn May Not Be for Everyone

I am not an expert on advertising using LinkedIn's pay per click (PPC) model. I haven't done any extensive research on it either but from a few articles that I have read, it may be a little expensive for some (relative to Facebook's PPC). If you are a local business that want to save a little of their cash up front that is starting out, then you may want to weigh your options or test out this LinkedIn's advertising once your business is profitable. I wouldn't recommend using this until then or UNLESS you know of a proven way to utilize its functionality for your business right away. Your returns might be better using their PPC platform when you consider the average annual income of a LinkedIn member.

I would love to know of any ways where advertising on LinkedIn can be done efficiently and effectively for any business. Please go to andrelvaughn.com and contact me so that I can share it with my community.

Simple Advice While Using LinkedIn

From my experience, LinkedIn members are some of the most helpful people on the entire social media sites. There is a professional etiquette that you must live by while on LinkedIn as well. Just be respectful and ask plenty of questions while exploring this awesome community and members will gladly help you with just about any relevant information. Do not spam your content all over LinkedIn and be sure to share and engage others content more than your own. Other people in your network will definitely take notice as well.

California Attorney Gets $12,000 in Referrals from LinkedIn!

An attorney from California named Mark Poniatowski got referrals from LinkedIn worth $12,000 by fixing his profile. The referrals came a few weeks after Poniatowski improved his LinkedIn page. He spent an hour fixing his LinkedIn profile and three hours connecting with people he knew professionally. He set aside 30 minutes, once a week, to build his network and engage through "content sharing." Poniatowski said that the site helped him keep track of position changes, set up introductions and research business decision-makers within his network.

Chapter 10

Twitter Can Be a Great Tool for Local Businesses

Twitter is possibly the best conversational social media site today. It can be a real microphone piece for your business or better yet...YOU! What I mean by that is brand recognition works great for 'BIG' brands better on Twitter (at least in my view) so I like to opt for having an account for myself to distribute content about my business. I am in no way saying that it couldn't work the other way around (because it does for major companies) but personal branding is my preference and works really well for local businesses.

Why does Personal Branding works better on Twitter?

I believe the great people on Twitter react more when there is a face attached to the conversation as oppose to an avatar of a "brand." I believe local businesses will thrive or get more interaction with potential customers better if the owner's face or image is uploaded as oppose to the businesses "logo." I know that it may sound silly and probably makes zero sense to most but you have to consider what Twitter is to fully grasp the concept.

What Exactly is Twitter?

Twitter is a micro blogging site where you can distribute a message up to 140 characters of text, photo or video content all over the world to people that are "following" your profile. Setting up your Twitter account is fairly simple to do. It's very similar to most of the other social networking sites so you should have little problem getting that done.

I like to follow relevant people or people that are potential customers in my niche for example I like to follow business owners and/or entrepreneurs. I find the people in my niche by going to the search bar to enter the keyword "business owner" or "entrepreneurs." You can navigate the search function rather easily and it lets you chose the type of content that you are looking for after you get results (people, photos, videos, etc.). Once I start clicking the "follow" button then I am adding these particular people in my Twitter network.

You can add or follow up to 1000 people per day. I recommend following 800 "targeted" people per day (I will tell you why as you read along).

Right Way to Engage on Twitter and a Quick Tip

Twitter is very similar to text messaging without the direct notification or your computer actually shaking off the table literally buzzing. You can get a notification but not the way you would with a text message. It functions as a conversational tool so you must have a natural conversation. The best way is to ask questions but do it with text and an image or video. You will see the difference and engagement will likely occur.

Within your Tweet be sure to use the symbol @ while targeting a particular person(s) while delivering your content or message (Tip: Never start a tweet out using @ as the first character because that person's followers will not see your message…you want all of their followers to see the message too). Sometimes I use multiple symbols of @ and try to find two or three people to seek information from or start a conversation.

Hashtags # have become very famous by using Twitter. Other social media sites such as Facebook, Instagram, Google Plus, Pinterest, Tumblr and a few others have adopted this very cool searchable symbol for their platforms. It is a way that your content is searched within Twitter. I highly recommend that you use hashtag #YourCity and #YourBusiness name on any and every Tweet that you send out. You will be glad that you did this later in the lifecycle of your business and use of Twitter.

It is very important that you respond to tweets because it is a conversation and you want to appear as human as possible. It carries you and your brand a long way when you say "Thanks @potential customer for the follow" or for whatever value that you received from the connection. This will show that person along with your community that you care about them as well.

The real benefit of Twitter is the retweet or RT which occurs when your tweet or content is redistributed. When this occurs, the message is seen through the streams of whomever that retweeted the content which makes it available to their followers. It can easily spread like a wildfire and become very popular. This is how content spreads about a local business and has the ability to go viral as well.

Wrong Way to Engage on Twitter & Other Social Sites

The biggest mistake on Twitter also occurs to be perhaps one of the worst for most businesses on just about any social media platform is trying to sell on every Tweet. I routinely scroll through all of the major social media sites that I am apart of and just shake my head in confusion at this.

It's the absolute wrong approach and it occurs far too often. People don't want to be sold to every time they go through their social feed which is why they don't buy often the vast majority of the time but yet it is a constant habit of many businesses that use social media.

As an owner of a local business or any kind of business, you should never sell all the time on your social accounts. Instead provide as much value as possible by giving as much information about your products and services that will help your customers or potential customers in determining rather to purchase or not. Ask questions and more importantly answer plenty of them also.

When Should I sell on Twitter or Any Social Site?

I just heard you say (or think), "When should I sell on Twitter or my other channels?" The answer is easy…very little and here is why: Social media networks are all public forums and many people are "listening" to your conversations so you should always be conscious of how potential customers may view you. The last thing that you want is to turn off someone or rub them the wrong way with the pressure of selling every time they see one of your tweets or posts. Your potential customers want to build trust if they never had your products or services. The best way for you to do that is by adding value and plenty of it first.

If you are a restaurant that does weekly specials and you want to get the word out on Twitter, then pick a strategy that works such as Tweet 5-6 times a day and only pick two days where you are getting the word out about your weekly specials during "peak" hours (time when people are on Twitter the most). Within those two days and those 5-6 tweets, only mention that special two or three times per those days. It may also be good practice to ramp up to 6-8 tweets on the days where business is the slowest. People understand what you are doing but you have to build trust with your brand by giving some sort of value to your potential customers and it certainly works on Twitter.

Previous Point about Followers

Earlier in this section I alluded to following 800 "targeted" or niche related members daily (for the first 30 days) instead of the allowed 1000 that Twitter limits your account to. The reason for doing so is that all of the followers will not follow you back. Just like the big boy search engines Google, Yahoo and Bing the social media sites are standalone search engines as well. Each are made up of their own algorithms or a step by step procedure to calculate a function. The algorithms let the "search" function operate in a way to give credence to the best quality user who either interacts the most and/or produces the highest quality of content.

This is why I am trying to deliver to you a very good understanding about the importance of engagement and quality content. It all works as a function to get potential customers to retweet or favor your content plus their followers can see the interactions and so. The entire landscape and process works as one when you consider the benefits of sharing on Twitter.

Quick Example of Twitter's Effect for an Antique Business

A New York Times article titled, "Marketing Small Businesses with Twitter" revealed how different local businesses are using Twitter. A few of the stories that were published in the piece were businesses that are in towns with very small populations such as a local store in Columbus, TX called Silver Barn Antiques. The owner of this shop is named Cynthia Sutton-Stolle and when she joined Twitter she noticed that people outside of her town were interested in her merchandise: "Twitter has been a real valuable tool because it's made us national instead of a little-bitty store in a little-bitty town." In addition, she stated that Twitter has been very instrumental to her business in finding suppliers as well.

Chapter 11

Keyword Placement for Social Media Channels

One of the most underrated things with any social media network is the importance of keyword placement. Three of the most searched websites on the web are Google, Yahoo and Bing. I will discuss how they are associated with keywords briefly so that you can see the importance of this for any local business that is using social media marketing.

People go on these platforms and search away 24 hours a day 7 days a week. Within the search engines mentioned, (about 2 to 7 days after you set up your account) sites like Google Plus, YouTube, Twitter and others will show in the results if searched. The reason the social media sites are so prevalent is because they are so powerful within the algorithms of these huge and very effective search engines. In other words, the domains (www.) are very strong because of the "social signals" or credence (trust) that the search engines give to social sites such as these. They get top priority and will often show up on the 1st page of search results.

A great source is to do keyword research by using the Google Keyword Planner. This "little piece" of web application is probably going to be one of your most valuable tools through your entire social media lifecycle. You can search any keyword related to your area of business and competition for the correct keywords. This tool has a variety of features and it is very easy to navigate. Do not make the mistake of not utilizing this very crucial tool for your local business!

Title and Description of Related Work

The title of any searchable item is invaluable. It doesn't matter what social media task that you are doing because the purpose is to use keywords where people will find what they are looking for within that search results. Without confusing those that are virtually new to these concepts, it's for SEO or Search Engine Optimization purposes (I won't dive too deep into SEO but these features make up the "outer crust" of it and its why keyword placement is so important). Basically, your local business will be found in the search engines a lot easier when someone searches your type of business, etc. when things such as the title is implemented.

Always put the keyword at the beginning of any title or as close to the beginning as you can. Here's an example: You are building a Pinterest board for related pins to your products or services. While filling out the description be sure to enter the main keyword at the beginning and enter it around two more times in the description to be safe. Make sure it looks natural so that you wouldn't be "keyword stuffing" or using the same keywords over and over.

Be Mindful of a Few Things

When you open a social media account make it very niche related. An example would be if you are a real estate agent in San Diego, CA and you are opening a Pinterest account, it wouldn't be a bad idea to see if the name "San Diego Real Estate Agent" (or something to that effect that is location based) is available. I actually prefer using the name of the business because of branding but every social network will not allow your account to be set up without an actual name. The reason for this is so that your local business can be found in the search engines like Google, Yahoo and Bing also for an added benefit.

Chapter 12

Facebook is One of the Best Marketing Tools in History

The title of this chapter is a big statement but it is so true for any local business. "...the Best Marketing...in History" sounds flashy, huh? I had to get your attention because Facebook garners a wealth of concentration for your business. It is a very true statement and CEO Mark Zuckerberg along with COO Sheryl Sandberg and the rest of their team knows it. For local businesses, Facebook could be like the second coming of the computerized cash register!

Seriously, if you are a local business or any business entrepreneur and you don't have a Facebook fan or business page then my question to you is What the (fill in the blanks respectfully of course) are you waiting on? You might be saying, "Ok Andre I am doing quite well without Facebook." My answer to you is simply, You can do better with it and a whole lot better than you think!

Whether you believe it or not, your friends either like what you like or you like what they like and so on. That's not to say that your friends eat chicken livers and you hate them or vice versa.

My point is your friends or even virtual friends have something in common with you whether you believe it or not. That is a fact in more cases than the alternative. "So what's your point, Andre?" And yes, this 2nd and/or 3rd person thing I am getting a real kick out of...HA...HA! But in all seriousness, when someone on Facebook likes, comments and obviously shares anything then their friends will see it as well. The more engagement that people have with a Facebook post, the more their friends will see it and more than likely do the same. It's not about guessing it is about human interaction and this is what happens on social network sites such as Facebook.

If you already have a fan or business page then at least you are at first base. My next few questions for you are how often are you posting content on Facebook? What are you posting (only text or photos and videos) and are you engaging or responding with your customer base? How often are you selling in your posts? These are key questions that you should have relevant answers to in developing a great Facebook strategy for your local business.

This is all a "science" sort of speak and you probably don't think so but how well are you currently doing randomizing your Facebook posts? That's not to say that you are likely not maximizing the full potential of Facebook but not even close in my humble opinion.

Just posting random content on Facebook will probably not cut it nor just posting only things about your business. This will have to be a strategic long term approach because Facebook will go through a series of algorithm changes as most of the top social media sites today so plan accordingly.

Helpful Tips for your Facebook Fan Page

Tip #1 You Must Post Consistently

Just as I said with YouTube and any of your social channels, you have to post consistently. For Facebook it means daily but not 15 times a day! If you post a lot daily then people will start "un-liking" your fan page and you will gain detractors. If you post 2-3 times a day of useful content then you will be on the right path but most certainly not more than that. I post often because I have a different business that caters to other businesses (B2B) but you may have a business that targets consumers (B2C) in your local area that will likely be a bit annoyed if they see constant updates in their newsfeed.

Tip #2 Three Mistakes that Most Local Businesses Make on Facebook

1) They start a page and never update it
2) They don't post images or videos of their products and services
3) Too much selling and not producing enough valuable content

Two Things that Should Open Your Eyes about Facebook

1) This first one is a No Brainer: over 1.5 Billion monthly users are on Facebook (at the time of publication 2016). Facebook has the largest population in the world behind China and India (if it was a country and is growing rapidly). Everyone or just about everyone is on Facebook. Newsflash: Your potential customers and current customers are likely using it and will buy from you consistently if you are offering value in your updates and offer great products and/or services. Why wouldn't you want to do the correct things for your business to flourish by using Facebook?

2) Facebook CEO Mark Zuckerberg has become one of the top marketers in the world. I always laugh or even chuckle whenever I hear him say how Facebook is "a place for people to connect with their friends." He has said this and many variations of it over and over many times he has spoken publicly. No one

admires and respects him for what he has created more than I do. But he steadily shows how far his brilliance as a marketer has become.

To better translate his message or what he is *REALLY* saying is that "I have over 1.5 Billion monthly active users in my network and I am going to take full advantage of it." I'm certainly not criticizing Zuckerberg but praising him for the platform that he and his team has built that is a true asset for many businesses around the world.

Quite naturally, he should flash those numbers in front of potential advertisers to generate revenue for his massive company. And as a local business owner or any business owner, you should take full advantage of this great social platform too.

What is so great about Facebook Advertising?

Facebook has a PPC or pay per click model that is designed for advertisers to set their own budgets (similar to Google but SO DIFFERENT) and allows marketers or local business owners to pay a credit each time their ad is clicked by a potential customer. If you want to spend $5 or $15 a day or more then you can do so with total control of your budget. The PPC model is cost effective for anyone who is trying to extend their reach and it gives businesses plenty of other options as well.

Here is the true genius of Facebook marketing and why I think it is the best model anywhere today: Facebook works with the best consumer data companies in the world. These companies gather consumer data and pair them with Facebook profiles to see what likely fits. In other words, they can take the consumer data and match them with every single thing that you and your "Facemates" liked, commented and shared. They then use the data to better segment and target possible leads within their advertising platform and the results are just stunning when you run the advertising campaign the proper way. Essentially you can go after new customers with a not so expensive budget.

Next time that you are reading your news feed on Facebook, start noticing "Suggested Post" or "Sponsored" which is one way that you can recognize a PPC campaign. You can take your business to new heights with this laser targeted approach of sharing offers for your products and services with prospects.

A Study about Facebook Marketing for Local Businesses

A great article from digiday.com reveals how Facebook is trying to encourage small businesses to use their advertising platform because of its pinpoint ad targeting accuracy. Here's what they found:

"A March 2014 study from BIA/Kelsey found that Facebook is the most popular media channel among small businesses. More than half (57.9 percent) of respondents said that they use Facebook to advertise their small business, with 43.2 percent saying they use newspapers. Sponsorships and Google were used by 37.9 percent of respondents, and email marketing was slightly less popular at 36.8 percent."

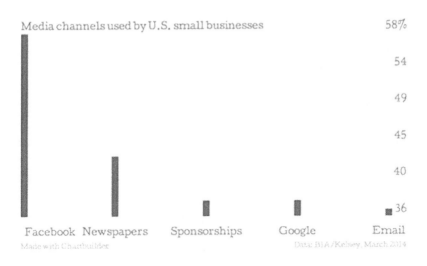

BIG Facebook Tip for Brick and Mortar Type Local Businesses

Having a brick and mortar business is great and can be very profitable if you set up your Facebook business page properly (you'll need to choose 'Local Business' for your Page's category and add your business address to the Page). You also need to do a search of your business (in Facebook's search box) to see if you have a 'Facebook Place Page' so that you can claim it. There is a link on that page which says "Is this your business." Click on it so that you can go through a short verification process to claim your page.

Facebook's Help Center says:

"If you find duplicate Pages for your business when you search for it, you may be seeing Pages for the locations people made when they checked in. Once must create an official Page for your business, you can claim and merge duplicates to keep the people who like your Page and check-ins in one place."

If a customer 'Check In' to your local business on Facebook from a mobile device, it can reach MANY other potential customers and give your local business a great boost! You may have a customer with 1,000 plus friends and their entire list will see it. What would this mean for your business if 10 customers checked in daily or even 20, 30, 40 or even 50 customers?

Why not promote 'Check In on Facebook' via a sign outside the window of your business and inside with a noticeable sign or at the tables assuming that you have a sit down type business? With the 'Check In on Facebook' sign you can also give something of value such as a discount or just add something that you are already giving away as an incentive. You will get better results when you ask your walk in customer to take action in return for something of value. This FREE tip alone can get you recurring business ESPECIALLY if used along with other 'location based' social media sites such as Twitter, Instagram and even Foursquare.

Chapter 13

Utilizing Other Resources to Help your Social Channels

There are many awesome resources that you should be using as a local business owner to help with your social channels. My favorite for many of my projects have been facilitated at Fiverr.com. It's a website were many of your tasks can be completed starting at $5. If you are in need of more "custom" things or want more tasks completed, then be sure to complete the entire format of the 'Gig' for more information. I have purchase things such as custom covers for my social media channels on other websites that I own, SEO tasks, etc.

It is very important to check for reviews and purchase 'Gigs' with ratings near or at 100%. I never purchase from a seller that has a below 98% rating under any circumstances. From my experience, that is a pretty good threshold when dealing with the vast number of sellers on Fiverr. If you ever have an issue with a seller, the Fiverr team is always willing to help you and resolve any issues.

One of the great things about posting to social media is there are many tools that can save you time. Some of the tools are FREE and some have paid versions as well. A few of the most widely used are HootSuite, Buffer, Post Planner and IFTTT ('If This Then That') to name a few.

With these tools you are able to do things such as syndicate and/or schedule (auto post) your content.

Helpful Resources for Creative Images and Other Tasks

When I post images on my social media channels I often times use Canva.com. You can set up a FREE account and watch the design tutorials (which are very easy to learn) so that you can get started. There are some advanced images that are priced very low so that you can take full advantage of the entire platform. Other places to get visual tasks done are at places like oDesk, Elance and 99 Designs for services that may cost a bit more but are very resourceful and professional.

Chapter 14

Simple & Effective Outsourcing to Build Your Social Media Team

One of my mantras is to "Work Smart and Minimize the Hard Part." I use that statement because that's how I truly feel about productivity. Why work hard when you may not be as good especially when you can simply outsource your social media tasks?

If you don't know that much about social media other than the basics or would like to know more information on outsourcing and building a small social media team as part of your business, then a great book that I recommend is "Virtual Freedom" by Chris Ducker. It will introduce you to the world of VA's or Virtual Assistants and is the best book that I have read on new business outsourcing. It's a must read and you will discover that it may also be a lot cheaper to use a virtual assistant to manage your social media tasks than you think.

Think about how efficient your local business would be if you had someone that was already experienced with different social media platforms (including the marketing side) to manage and run your campaigns and channels! Your business could grow exponentially because your focus would now be on other parts of your operation rather than putting time and effort in something that may take away from other aspects of your business. This may not be a viable option for everyone but it may also be something that your business simply can't live without to grow and sustain over time.

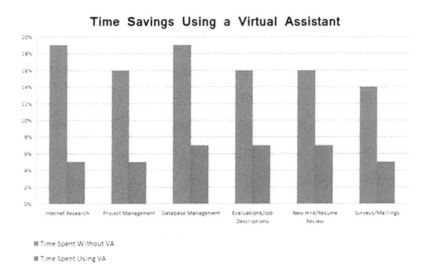

Time Savings Using a Virtual Assistant

■ Time Spent Without VA
■ Time Spent Using VA

Alternative to Using a Virtual Assistant

You may already have someone that is part of your staff who is an excellent fit for your social media team. If that's the case then by all means do what is best for your business. Be sure this person is learning all the time to staying up to date on the ever changing world of social media. Remember this is a technology and it moves with lightning appeal.

Another alternative to using a VA is by hiring someone outside of your company that has experience. This could be a very useful option for your business but is by far the most expensive. It can work for you if you have the budget to do so and may help your business even if the employee is part time.

The final alternative is the person that you see in the mirror daily...YOU! If you choose to manage your social media platforms, who's to say that your business can't be a success? My only concern is as your business grows, how long will your business be sustainable and how will you scale if it's not growing? Just a rhetorical or shall I say a "loaded" question. Why go through the rigors of not focusing on more important things in your business with the exception that you are planning for someone other than yourself to manage your social media efforts? Ultimately, the decision is yours to do what is best for your business.

Chapter 15

3 Simple Tips to Determine Which Social Media Channel Works for Your Business

Using every social media channels that is available may not be the best thing for your business. To attempt this would be a complete waste of your time and efforts. I have three actionable tips that will help your decision in finding out which platform works for you.

Tip #1

Ask your customers do they use social media and which ones are they using the most. You will likely notice their mobile device in their hand or nearby in which they access the platform as well.

Tip #2

Go online to see what social media sites your top 3 to 5 competitors are using (assuming this applies to your business) in your local market.

Tip #3

Find out what elements of social media that your competitors are using.

In business, every relationship is key and even bigger with your current customers. They are already purchasing from you so they look at you as a trusted source. Your goal is to get 'social word of mouth' and get them to share their experience of your local business with their network of family and friends. Once you find out where your current customers are then you can target your audience better and go to the source where potential customers are hanging out.

Inside Social Media Marketing and what Works for Your Business

I am of the belief that certain trends tell the majority of the story in where anything is headed in any business. Local businesses will be more successful and profitable when they understand social media marketing along with the major search engines and mobile usage facilitating everything.

Have you ever looked around especially in a public place and notice everyone holding their mobile phones in their hands and pecking away? What about being at your local coffee shop or other places and see someone on a mobile tablet so focused on the task at hand? I can guess that many are on social media or on its search engine looking for information (I didn't forget about texting too...HA...HA...). When potential customers are in your place of business and using a mobile device, it is crucial that they are instructed to do something so they can keep up with the latest updates about your products or services through a social media channel or mobile campaign.

Google Plus, YouTube and even Pinterest all weigh heavily within the search results for the Big 3 (Google, Yahoo and Bing). Use any of the three & do a quick search on just about anything and you should not be surprised to see an element of the top social media sites lurking in the search results.

What about Facebook and the others discussed previously? Facebook's functionality alone and what it can do to target potential leads is a no brainer to use but you will find more fan pages in the search results more than anything because Facebook tells the search engines to 'No Follow' most of its website. This is why you only see few results with its domain name attached unless you are searching for something or someone specific using the Big 3 (Google, Yahoo and Bing). They have designed it to keep their users within their platform for all of your needs which is brilliant when you consider the entire landscape of the social media giant.

Instagram, Tumblr and Pinterest all have their place because of the visual nature of all three social media sites. If you have an active account on any social media channel, notice how many images and videos that you see.

This also heavily applies to Twitter because you have more engagement from a tweet when there is a visual such as an image or a video. Take advantage of these for your business NOW before your competition does.

What about LinkedIn? I didn't forget about this one but most local businesses completely ignore LinkedIn because it's a 'professional' social networking site. That alone will shrug a few people away but don't let it deter your efforts and potential growth of your business. It's certainly not for everyone to use but how can any service business not utilize it to some degree by targeting people that are already in their own backyard?

If you are a food truck owner, why wouldn't you want to take full advantage of the network of 'attorneys' in the huge office area that you are serving for on a particular day? You have an aspiring restaurant that is fairly new and you want to offer workers in the busiest office building(s) in your area an incentive or discount on your awesome specials on a particular day of the week during lunch time. The scenarios can go on forever but if enough information is gathered you could make a huge impact using LinkedIn.

3 Simple Perspectives on Social Media Marketing

1) Consistency equals Simplicity: Posting with regularity, the proper way by using images and videos with mobile in mind (location based features) keeps you on the right track

2) Pay per click or PPC is an excellent model for any local small business because you set the budget and can stop or pause a campaign at any time

3) Outsourcing can be your ticket for growth and success because it allows you to hire a virtual assistant who is already trained in the task of social media marketing thus allowing a business owner time to focus on other parts of his or her business

I'm not sure if that helped you or not but my ears are always up in the air to see what is working or not in the world of social media marketing. Watching and listening to what is going on at all times for local small businesses through social media in the most simplistic way is what I love doing.

Read this for Your Benefit!

Many local small businesses are absolutely CRUSHING IT using social media marketing because they understand many of the principles and were brave enough to know there limitations . Many of these businesses are doing other great things in their communities as well. I can't help but to notice it because as part of my research it's my duty to notice as much as I can and to spread my findings of these things for people like yourself that are by far smarter than I am.

A few words to the wise local business owner or entrepreneur (which is you):   Please be smarter than I was in my first business & do not accept being average or lazy because I had a steady income stream and complacency set in. My ears were shut to the 'Next Big Thing' and to a degree the 'Right Things.' Cognitively I was not fully up to par because I was WAY too comfortable with getting by and not focusing on growing my business. I don't want to see any of you in the same predicament that I was in. The 'Next Big Thing' is here and most local business owners are not taking advantage of this GIGANTIC opportunity to use social media marketing in a useful and simplistic way within their local areas.

I have stated a few times previously that your customers are using social media daily and way more often than you may think. People are more likely to try things that their friends recommend (word of mouth). This has been proven time and time again with social media and through traditional marketing.

I have provided more than enough information to give you a simple understanding of how social media marketing functions and how you can take advantage of a few effective tips for your local business to advance and grow.

Remember this book was written for local business owners (or small to medium sized) to simplify social media marketing and not intended as a publication to skyrocket a Fortune 500 company with the information that has been presented. However, I believe the message delivered along with the different strategies and tactics can help other type of businesses around the world as well. But for the small to medium sized business owner or entrepreneur, these current times are an opportunity of a lifetime for you. Good luck and until the next time…Thank you all!

GET THIS NOW!

Thank you for purchasing and reading but I have more for you. Get your FREE BONUS as a token of my appreciation and further help your small business succeed with simple social media marketing.

-5 PART VIDEO COURSE

-DOWNLOADABLE REPORT

-PRIVATE COMMUNITY

-EXCLUSIVE ACCESS TO THE AUTHOR

Visit the link below to get access to your **FREE Bonus!**

www.socialmediasimplemarketing.com

One Last Thing…

As you start to implement the different tips and strategies that will make your local small business a success, I ask that you go rate this book and share your thoughts on **Facebook** and **Twitter**. If you think that other business owners would get any value from this book, I would be more than grateful if you recommended it to them as well. Furthermore, I would be astounded if you posted a **Review on Amazon** or any other retailer where you may have purchased this book.

Thanks again and to your complete success,

Andre L. Vaughn
andrelvaughn.com

About the Author

Andre L. Vaughn is a local business marketing & social media strategist who is passionate about helping businesses understand and utilize the simple solutions of social media, mobile, video and email marketing along with web development platforms. He is a graduate of the University of Missouri-St. Louis with a B.S. in Information Systems and a B.S. in Business Administration.

Andre loves spending countless hours with his family and friends along with strategically planning the next move. An avid admirer of sports, he loves following professional American football and the "Sweet Science" of boxing. Only the beginning of the journey, he wants and continues to provide value to small businesses around the world so they can have success and enjoy different ways in which business is done through simple 'emerging' marketing solutions.

Resources

andrelvaughn.com (My Blog)

pewresearch.org/data-trend/media-and-technology/social-networking-use

pewinternet.org/fact-sheets/social-networking-fact-sheet

comscore.com

google.com/business/placesforbusiness

locbox.com/success/bodycentre-wellness-spa

socialmediaexaminer.com

chippewa.com/business/businessreport/columns/marketing-leveraging-visually-oriented-social-media-tools/article_2d28c571-25f8-5f54-aabd-8ae23232e7d9.html

youtube.com/user/smithpots

pinterestmarketingplans.com

usatoday30.usatoday.com/video/local-businesses-using-instagram-to-entice-shoppers/2238260641001

moutonco.org/blog/2012/08/4-killer-ways-to-use-instagram-for_22.html (Monton Consulting)

corp.wishpond.com (Wishpond Marketing)

businessdayonline.com/2014/05/business-lawyer-gets-12000-worth-of-referrals-via-linkedin

digiday.com/platforms/facebook-twitter-courting-small-businesses

nytimes.com/2009/07/23/business/smallbusiness/23twitter.html?_r=0

constantcontact.com

aweber.com

canva.com

fiverr.com

odesk.com

elance.com

chrisducker.com

virtualfreedombook.com

mycrowd.com/blog/get-boost-increase-productivity-grow-business-save-time-virtual-assistant

hugeinc.com/ideas/report/social-roi

statista.com/statistics/272014/global-social-networks-ranked-by-number-of-users